The Lost Art of Faith Righteousness

Rediscover How Believing Leads to Receiving

© Copyright 2022 Daniel Newton, GP Publishing

www.graceplaceredding.com

Contributing authors: The Grace Place Leadership Team

ISBN: 978-1-957601-05-2

"For if, by the trespass of the one man, death reigned through that one man, how much more will those who receive God's abundant provision of grace and of the gift of righteousness reign in life through the one man, Jesus Christ!"

- Romans 5:17

Resources by Daniel Newton and Grace Place Ministries:

Truth in Tension: 55 Days to Living in Balance

Immeasurable: Reviewing the Goodness of God

Never Give Up: The Supernatural Power of Christlike Endurance

The Lost Art of Discipleship

The Lost Art of Discipleship Workbook

The Lost Art of Perseverance

All Things

It Is Finished

GP Music: Beginnings – Worship Album

For more information on these books
and other inspiring resources, visit us at
www.GracePlaceMedia.com

Table of Contents

Introduction

Let's face it. The world is having a massive identity crisis. We live in a generation that defines itself based on feelings and preferences. Truth, history, values, science, and even gender have been made relative to what *you* want it to be. To many, there is not *the* truth, just *your* truth.

Don't like history? Rewrite it. Don't like the sex you were born with? Change it. There's not a gender you like? Make up your own. You are the god of your own life, and your world can be defined in whatever terms you wish. Theology, the knowledge of God, has been replaced with "me-ology." We have become addicted to ourselves, and it's wreaking havoc on a massive scale. Studies show that depression, hopelessness, suicide, drug addiction, and family dysfunction are at all-time highs. Clearly, the worldly wisdom we're being sold as "liberating" and "great" is not so great after all.

Since 2008, I have run a discipleship ministry through which I have fathered and discipled young adults as they grow into who God has called them to be. When I start meeting with people, they often want to discuss their problems with me. They come to me with a laundry list of struggles and sins that they no longer want in their lives. I tell them that the real issue isn't looking at porn, choosing distraction, reacting in anger, partnering with self-hatred, fear, stealing, overeating, or anything else. The real issue, which all the others stem from, is not understanding who they are and what they were created to be. The answers to those questions are not found in altering your identity based on how you feel each day. That may be the world's way of doing things, but it's devoid of real transformation. The true answer is found where it always has been: Jesus' life, death, and resurrection.

The Western Church today has reduced the Gospel down to a children's story we tell on Easter and Christmas. Jesus is either the little baby in the center of the nativity or the pale-looking figure etched into our stained glass windows. Many who talk about the importance of a personal relationship with Jesus fail to explain what that actually means. The Gospel has been watered down into a feel-good message that pushes all hope of actual transformation to the future. You may believe God wants good for you, but are you pushing it off to a time or place outside your reach?

If you believe that Jesus died on the Cross for the sole purpose of getting you to heaven, then ultimately, death is your savior. You're expecting death to be the doorway to the manifest blessings of God. You've reduced salvation to a waiting game until you can finally punch the clock and enter the "great by and by." However, the Gospel the disciples preached was radically different, and it changed the course of the entire world.

The good news of the Gospel is that we have been reconciled to God. Through the death and resurrection of His only Son, a new reality has been unveiled. The door has been opened for each of us to access the righteousness of God through faith in Jesus Christ. We call this gift "faith righteousness," but unfortunately, living in it has become a lost art. What happened at the Cross was far more than just attaining a ticket to heaven.

The Cross is the place where you and your issues died with Christ so that you could be born again as a *new creation*. When this becomes the foundation of your identity, you will never be the same. This truth of faith righteousness is the centerpiece of the Gospel. Sadly, the majority of the modern Church has lost touch with what Jesus really paid for, and that's what we are about to rediscover in the pages to come.

These truths are more than just theological statements but are the doorway into a bigger life than you have ever imagined. If you allow this message, the *good* news, to become the way in which you interact with the Lord, it will change your life forever. I've seen what I'm about to share with you change the lives of countless people all over the world. I pray that you read this book with an open mind and open heart so that you may rediscover *The Lost Art of Faith Righteousness*. This is the message Jesus came to release to the world. And it's better than you think.

Chapter One

The Full Package of Salvation

I once led a healing service in Mexico where the church was erupting with praise. All across the room, people were being healed by the power of the Gospel. In the midst of the miracles, I noticed a man on the front row that was being tormented by demons. I stopped focusing on healing for a moment and took authority over the room saying, "Right now, I release peace in Jesus' name." As I stepped back into the flow of the meeting, I suddenly got a word of knowledge.

I walked up to the man and asked, "Sir, do you have pain in your head?"

"Yes—how do you know that?" he responded.

"God told me, and He wants to heal you. Can I pray for you?" I laid my hands on him and began to pray. All of this was taking place in front of a crowd of at least one hundred-fifty people.

"Okay, how are you feeling now?" I asked.

Usually, when I pray for someone to be healed, they will respond by saying either "I feel the same," "I feel partially better," or "Oh my gosh, the pain is gone!" That pretty much sums up the normal responses I receive. However, this guy didn't say any of those. Instead, he looked at me and said, "I feel hatred."

I said, "Okay, we can deal with that." After a brief word with the pastor, I gave the meeting over to my intern. The pastor and I then invited the man to another room. I sat him down and asked, "Do you know Jesus?"

"No."

"Do you want to be free from this?"

"Yes."

"Do you want to receive the full package of salvation that Jesus died for on the cross to give you?

"Yes, I do."

"You deal with violence and anger, don't you?"

"Yes," he replied, as he suddenly began twitching and manifesting demons.

"Look at me. You don't have to deal with this anymore. When you choose to give your life to Jesus, you're choosing to give up your life, and you're choosing to accept His life. Everything you know is going to change."

I spent the next ten minutes teaching him what I'm about to tell you. We went through the whole Gospel: what it means to be co-crucified and co-buried with Christ, then co-raised and co-seated with Him. I said, "You are choosing to commit your life to Him and become a son of God. When you're a son of God, the enemy has no hold on you anymore. As you make this decision right now, everything as you know it is going to change. The bible says if any man is in Christ he is a new creation all the old things have passed away, all things have become new. There will be no hatred, there will be no violence, there will be no anger, and there will be no pain. Surrender your life to Him. Give Him everything you are, and He will give you everything He is."

Do you know what happened after ten minutes of preaching to him? He commit his life to follow Jesus. As he did, the demons left him, the pain left him, and his entire countenance changed. All of this happened in a period of about 15 or 20 minutes. He got saved, he got healed, and he got delivered. Everything about him changed. And you know what's even better? I got an email a few months later from the pastors of his church. They told me he joined Youth With A Mission Discipleship Training School. This man will never be the same again.

The power this man experienced firsthand is available to you. The righteousness of God in Christ Jesus restored him. Every sin, every issue, and every demon that exists could never change who he now is in Christ. That is what this book is all about: identifying yourself in the righteousness of Jesus Christ.

One of the greatest problems we deal with in the Church today is, ironically, *how* we deal with our problems. Our response to sin and approach to handling failure needs to change. What we don't realize is that everything comes down to identity. We need to learn that we don't actually have all these different problems; we just have one. Struggling with sin? It's an identity problem. Struggling with anger? It's an identity problem. Struggling with pornography? It's an identity problem. If you're struggling with jealousy, fear, or insecurity, you guessed it—each of these are ultimately an identity problem. You need to learn who you have become in Christ Jesus. I believe that if you base your doctrine and your belief system on what you are about to read, it will change your life forever.

"For I am not ashamed of the gospel of Christ, for it is the power of God to salvation for everyone who believes, for the Jew first and also for the Greek. For in it the righteousness of God is revealed from faith to faith; as it is written, "The just shall live by faith."

– Romans 1:16-17

The word "Gospel" means "good news." If it's not good news, it's not the Gospel. Whenever you hear something that is not good news, what is the first thing that should come to your mind? That it's not the Gospel! Anything in my life that isn't good news doesn't get to have the final say in how I think or what I decide to do. I don't accept something that's not good news because it's not the Gospel.

The word "salvation" comes from the root word *sozo,* which means "saved, healed, delivered, set free, and prosperous." In other words, salvation is a full package deal. When you truly believe the Good News, it will bring the full package of *sozo* into your life. When you believe in the power of God, you get the fullness of what He paid for.

What I explained to the man in Mexico is so much more than just a prayer for him to pray as an entry point to Christianity. I told him about coming into a relationship with God, and it completely transformed his life.

What's the problem with the Gospel we have preached in the Western Church? For one, we make it about ourselves. We make it about what *we* need to do. So what is the Gospel? It is the power of *God.* Not the power of *you.* When you believe the Gospel, it brings the full power, the full package of salvation. It reconciles an everlasting bond between the Father and a lost child. Now you can fully rely on a God who gave everything He has to possess you as His own.

"For by grace you have been saved through faith, and that not of yourselves; it is the gift of God, not of works, lest anyone should boast."

– Ephesians 2:8-9

What we have to understand is that Jesus didn't die to give us a better set of rules to follow. God didn't send His Son to simply edit the existing law and make it more bearable. Jesus Christ established something entirely new, something that could not be earned by being good enough or taken away as punishment for failing to live up to it. Jesus came to establish what the Bible calls *grace.* By its very nature, grace is impossible to earn and something we will never deserve. Ephesians 2 calls it the *gift* of God. There's no way we could ever brag about deserving God's goodness because He chose to be good to us apart from our actions and works!

"For Christ is the end of the law for righteousness to everyone who believes."

– Romans 10:4

God has chosen to bless and unconditionally love us for all time. Do you want miracles in your life? The supernatural? Healing and deliverance? Provision? Joy and peace? The love of God and all the good He has to offer? If you are in Christ, you are qualified for all of that *outside* of your own performance! What you can do on your own to become righteous is no longer even taken into account!

Under the Old Covenant, if you wanted to be called "righteous," you had to act righteously. The problem was that God's standard for what He called "righteous" was *perfect*. It wasn't just above average; you had to keep the whole Law down to the letter or be guilty of breaking every part of it. It was pass or fail. And if you failed, there were more laws (sacrifices of doves, goats, bulls, and lambs) to ensure everything was atoned for.

However, the good news is that God never intended for us to be able to accomplish the Law without His help. In fact, some of the times you see God the most frustrated with the Israelites, His chosen people, were when they thought they could keep the Law without depending on Him. To think you're able to please God without His help is a form of deception—a dangerous misunderstanding of our created purpose.

During the time the epistles were written, there was a group of people called the Judaizers who believed in Jesus as their Lord and Savior. But, there was one thing they didn't believe Him to be: their righteousness.

Many believers have this same belief system today. They think, *Sure, Jesus, I believe you are Lord, but I still have to work for my righteousness. Jesus, yes, you're my Lord and Savior, but I still have to work, earn, and perform to be righteous.*

It's time to let go of our perceived need to prove ourselves to God and accept that He has already made up His mind about us. In Jesus, God has chosen once and for all to call us righteous. Salvation has been given by God as a free gift. It's absolutely free, and the only way we can restrict its benefits is by trying to earn them.

At this point, you may be asking, "Why is it so important to believe that I am righteous? What's the purpose?" The reason this is such a vital topic is that the Body of Christ is living condemned, discouraged, and hopeless. There is a startling lack of power and transformation in the common Christian. Most people just think that's the way it is. Anyone with a biblical understanding of the New Covenant would attest that God paid for more. Why am I not experiencing it? I would argue that most people are not believing in their righteous state.

And why would that matter? Because if you do not believe you are righteous, clean, and new, you will not pursue an intimate relationship with God. Without connection with God, including an awareness of Christ IN YOU, you will never rise to the occasion and let Christ out. You will always reduce your potential to the level of your last mistake.

God has made us righteous, not just because it sounds good, but because He wants a deep relationship with each one of us. The only way we can have that relationship is by being 100% pure and clean. But guess what? We already are 100% pure and clean by His blood! That's what all this is about: restoring connection with God so we can rise up and be the men and women of God He has always created us to be.

As we are transformed, the people and places around us will be changed. Our families, present and future, will reap the benefits of a life of faith righteousness and union with Jesus. Our workplaces will change for the better. Our neighborhoods, our cities, our nations, and all of creation will rejoice at the sons and daughters of God walking in the fullness of their righteous identities.

Chapter Two

Mercy and Grace

Imagine that you're driving a car and in a rush to your destination. Then, suddenly, you see the lights of a police car in your rearview mirror. You are being pulled over, and you know you deserve it. You know the speed limit is at least 25mph slower than you were going. However you were late and needed to make it to your meeting on time. The police officer could take your license if he wanted to. Whatever penalty he's giving you is justified. There's no way to argue your way out of this one.

You pull over and then roll down your window as he walks up.

He asks, "Do you have any idea how fast you were going just now?"

"Yes, sir," you say. "Way too fast."

"Way too fast," he echoes. "Any particular reason you found it appropriate to drive 95 miles per hour in a 70 zone?"

"I, um, was late?" It sounded like such a good justification a few minutes ago, but now it sounds foolish.

"You were late? You understand I have the authority to revoke your license for reckless driving, right? Was being on time *that* worth it to you?"

"No, sir."

The officer stares at you in silence for an uncomfortable amount of time. "Here's what I'm going to do," the officer says. "I ought to take your license, but it would mean a ton of paperwork for me and a nightmare for you. So, I'm going to let you go."

Your ears perk up, and you lift your head.

"Wait," you stammer, "you are? As in... completely?"

"Yes, I am. Completely. I will not be taking your license. I won't even give you a ticket. Just do me a favor: drive safely, and don't *ever* do something like this again."

What the officer just gave you was mercy, not grace. Mercy is deserving punishment, but being forgiven anyway. It is, in short, *not* getting what you *do* deserve. If you are caught breaking the law, you deserve punishment. If you speed, you deserve a ticket. If you steal, you deserve to go to jail. To deserve a ticket and not get one is mercy. If you deserve to go to jail and you are given freedom, it is an expression of mercy.

"Who is a God like you, who pardons sin and forgives the transgression of the remnant of his inheritance? You do not stay angry forever but delight to show mercy."
– Micah 7:18 (NIV)

Whenever I talk to people about grace, the question almost inevitably comes up: isn't it dangerous to give people grace because it lets them off the hook for the bad things they have done? Won't that just lead to more sin? It seems like a logical question to ask, but it comes from a misunderstanding of the difference between grace and mercy.

Grace goes far beyond mercy because it gives you what you *don't* deserve and could never deserve. It is a gift of unearned, unconditional favor. It is a power that will change you from the inside out. To treat grace as the same thing as mercy is to completely misunderstand both.

It is just as foolish to suggest that having too much grace *enables* sin. "Better watch out for that grace stuff unless you want sin to run rampant in your church." No! You want as much grace in your church as you can possibly get because grace is the supernatural power of God to live out what He commands. Grace is far more offensive to the mind and far more supernatural. To illustrate what this looks like, let's jump back into the story:

"Here's what I'm going to do," the officer says. "I ought to take your license, but it would mean a ton of paperwork for me and a nightmare for you. So, I'm going to let you go."

Your ears perk up, and you lift your head.

"Wait," you stammer, "you are? As in... completely?"

"Yes, I am. Completely. I will not be taking your license. I won't even give you a ticket."

"Wow! That's amazing, I don't even know what to—"

"I wasn't finished," the officer cuts in. "Not only am I not going to give you a ticket or take your license, but I want you to take this spare uniform, badge, and gun. You will have all of my authority to protect, empower, and bring justice. Anything I have the power to do, you are now empowered to do as well."

You look down at the uniform, badge, and gun in your hands in disbelief.

"I don't understand," you say. "I don't deserve this. I broke the law. I was speeding and driving recklessly. I'm a lawbreaker, not a police officer. You can't do this!"

The officer shrugs and smiles. "You're right. You don't deserve it. But I did it anyway. It's my gift to you, and my decision is final." He turns to walk toward his car, adding, "Hope you have a nice day!"

The officer waves as he drives away, leaving you speechless.

In our modern-day minds, this ending to the story makes no sense. There is no scenario where a police officer would pull someone over for breaking the law, withhold the punishment they deserved, and then proceed to give them the authority to enforce and administer justice. It's enough to be let off the hook for doing something wrong that was deserving of punishment. To go beyond that and give power and authority to someone who was caught in the act of breaking the law just wouldn't happen.

Yet that's exactly what Jesus did for us. He released us from our transgressions by *becoming* sin itself. He took our place and gave us His righteousness instead. He gave us mercy by sparing our punishment and made us right with God. And His grace has transformed us into ambassadors of His Kingdom.

In John 8, we find the story of the adulterous woman. Jesus was teaching in the temple when a group of men dragged a guilt-ridden woman before Him. They were more than ready to put her to death, and according to the Law of Moses, they were justified to do so. But Jesus flipped the scene upside-down. There are many powerful truths in this story, but I want to draw your attention to how Jesus interacts with the woman after those who condemned her left. The woman in the situation was guilty. She had been caught in the act of adultery, so there was no defending her actions. Watch what Jesus does:

> *"...He said to her, 'Woman, where are those accusers of yours? Has no one condemned you?' She said, 'No one, Lord.' And Jesus said to her, 'Neither do I condemn you; go and sin no more.'"*
> *– John 8:10-11*

Jesus' response to the woman reveals both the mercy and grace of God. *Neither do I condemn you.* In this statement, Jesus releases mercy and forgiveness to the woman. She was guilty but not condemned. According to the Law, she deserved the judgment and condemnation that came along with her actions. She deserved death on the spot. Jesus gave her something she did not deserve in that moment: mercy and forgiveness. She had committed a sin but was not going to face judgment for it. If Jesus had stopped there, this would have been a great day in her life. She was spared! She wasn't going to be stoned!

But Jesus did not stop there.

"Go and sin no more."

In what was likely one of the lowest moments of this woman's life, she was given a gift she could never earn and would never deserve: the liberating grace of God. Some interpret "Go and sin no more" as "don't do that again." But this wasn't an offhand comment that Jesus made. This was a commission from the mouth of the Son of God. Anytime Jesus tells us to do something, it always carries with it the *power* to do it.

This command to "go and sin no more" goes far beyond the limits of mere mercy and forgiveness. In these five words, Jesus gave the woman the power to do something impossible.

It is possible for us to show mercy to one another, but only God can give us grace. Only God has the power to end the cycle of sin and destruction in our lives. For Jesus to say this to the woman was just as radical as a police officer handing you his badge after pulling you over for speeding. It wasn't a mere commandment. It was an impartation of power. The woman now carried the ability, the *grace*, to live righteously.

"But God, who is rich in mercy, because of His great love with which He loved us, even when we were dead in trespasses, made us alive together with Christ (by grace you have been saved)"
- Ephesians 2:4-5

Jesus took us when we were lawbreakers and sinners. He forgave us, gave us a new heart, and then empowered us with His own Spirit to go and carry out His will on the earth! We now walk with the authority and power of the Holy Spirit, releasing heaven on earth everywhere we go. It took an act of great mercy to forgive us of all our sins and trespasses. However it took an even greater work of grace to make us like Himself. God was not willing to stop at simply showing mercy. He empowered us to be like Jesus through grace.

The standard for living is no longer just trying to avoid sin. The standard is now to walk in the image of your Maker. As you receive His grace, you will receive the power you need to fulfill the calling of God on your life. One pastor I know emphasizes, "Grace is two sides to the same coin: the unconditional favor of God *and* the power to transform." It says, "I love you, even in your worst mess," but it also says, "You don't have to stay there because I've given you the power to change."

Chapter Three

The Truth About our Faith Heroes

One day, I was watching TV, and there was a man preaching about intimacy with the Lord. This guy is well-known in Christian circles. If I told you his name, you would recognize it. While I was watching, he kept advertising a book he had written about intimacy with God. He had these little infomercials every ten minutes throughout his message. What's crazy is that his book is one of the best-selling books in the Christian world today. Countless people have read his book.

Even before his book came out, he was a famous songwriter who wrote many of the songs we sing today. Talk about an anointed man of God!

The interesting thing is that I know quite a bit about this author. I know the details going on behind the scenes, and aspects of his personal life were a mess. I know that he made several horrible decisions. He's been unfaithful to his wife. He's stabbed people in the back to get where he is. His family fell apart, and his children don't want anything to do with him.

He hardly seems like the kind of person you'd want teaching you about intimacy with God.

They won't broadcast any of that on Christian TV, but they're selling this book that he wrote anyway. Isn't it crazy that millions of people are buying a book on intimacy with God written by a man who is in infidelity and has made sinful, horrible decisions? Don't you think it's time we start living what we're preaching? Isn't it time we stop listening to people who are hypocrites?

Do you want to know who the guy is? Do you want to know what the book is?

His name is David, and the book is Psalms.

Of course, I put this story into our modern context, seeing that David lived over 2,000 years ago. But I want you to stop and think about this practically. All I did was give you vague specifics about David's life. We look up to him and his commitment to the Lord, but if David were alive today and he did what he did to Bathsheba and Uriah, how would we treat him? We would destroy him, we would crucify him, and we would tear him to shreds on the news, social media, and in Christian magazines. Yet God calls him a man after His own heart (see 1 Sam. 13:14). Our problem today is that any time someone falls or fails, we judge and condemn them.

I hate to break it to you, but most of the people we celebrate as heroes in the faith were not great people. In the Bible, you'll find their stories are a little more colorful and messy than you remember them being in Sunday school. These people were rough and rugged. I encourage you to read through the stories of the heroes of the faith that we so highly honor and respect and compare your life to theirs. Tell me, have you ever cheated someone out of their entire inheritance? Have you ever trafficked a member of your family into slavery? Have you ever murdered someone or had someone murdered? Have you ever committed adultery? These are just a few of the things you'll find in the stories of our heroes from the Bible.

Let's take Abraham, for example. He did not have a righteous lifestyle. He made some crazy and foolish decisions—in fact, probably more than most of us. Have you ever given your wife away to a king? Abraham did. And to be clear, this wasn't some kind of accidental, "Oops, I forgot for a moment I was married to my wife, Sarah. Sorry for the misunderstanding," kind of situation. He did this to save his own neck at her expense. To make it worse, he did it *twice!*

And yet, even in spite of this, Abraham was still called "righteous." That is the amazing power of God's grace. He sets aside our own qualifications and disqualifications to judge us simply on whether or not we believe we have found favor with God. The truly remarkable fact about Abraham was that he wasn't even born again! Jesus hadn't even died on the Cross! However he believed that something was available, and when he believed, the bridge was built between a future reality and his present one. He experienced righteousness that came apart from living a perfect life.

Like Abraham, we have to get to the place where we allow ourselves to connect with the truth and let the truth set us free. The simple fact is that if we don't believe the truth, nothing will change. You can read this book a thousand times over, and it won't do anything for you until the revelation becomes personal.

In John 8:31-32, Jesus speaks to the Jews who had believed in Him: "If you abide in My word" (ESV) or "hold to my teachings" (NLT) or "remain faithful to my teachings" (NIV), "you are my disciples indeed. And you shall know the truth and the truth shall make you free." They first believed and then, because they believed, continued to follow what He had taught them. Jesus said this would open them up to experiencing truth and freedom. Faith is what changes your life!

Any time you ever feel condemned for something you've done, look at David, Abraham, or Peter, and think, "Wow, wait a second. If God could use these broken people to accomplish mighty things, imagine what he could do with me!"

Peter denied him three times, and Jesus commissioned him to build His Church! Yet, when we do something wrong, we think it's the end of the world. "That's it; that was the last straw. I've really done it now." Why do we think that way? Because we're living under guilt, shame, and condemnation. We aren't seeing our situation with the same lens of mercy through which God sees. We're predicting our future without factoring in God's ability to redeem, restore, and revitalize.

In Hebrews 11, many of these imperfect Old Testament heroes are referenced. They are depicted in the noblest and most honorable light as men and women who lived by faith and were used by God to bring glory to His name. Nowhere in those pages does the author mention their compromises or failures because the Holy Spirit's perspective is one of mercy and redemption.

Where we only see a broken vessel, God sees an object of His glory and a trophy of grace. Imagine how different their stories would end if those heroes punished or condemned themselves for their flaws rather than receiving God's mercy and persevering?

In the Body of Christ today, when people feel guilty for what they've done, they often think they're being convicted by the Holy Spirit when, in reality, it's the enemy! The Bible even says the devil comes as an angel of light (see 2 Cor. 11:14). The enemy today is masquerading himself as the Holy Spirit, trying to convict the Church of sin. In reality, it is the accuser of the brethren releasing guilt, shame, and condemnation on God's people. Well-meaning Christians are allowing themselves to be beaten over the head with their mistakes and failures, disqualifying themselves from all that God has for them in life. God doesn't want that for you. He doesn't treat you that way.

Scripture doesn't say that it's God's guilt, shame, and condemnation that leads us to repentance. These things don't belong to God at all. If you're hoping you can be shamed into breakthrough and freedom, get ready to be very disappointed. The only thing guilt and shame will empower in your life is more guilt, more shame, and more sin. It's His *kindness* that leads us to repentance and causes our minds to be transformed (see Rom. 2:4). Remember that the Gospel is *good news*, so if what you're experiencing isn't good, it's not the Gospel!

If you are experiencing condemnation, it's because you don't understand why Jesus came. God is not in the business of condemning people. Jesus said, "For God did not send His Son into the world to condemn the world, but that the world through Him might be saved" (John 3:17). God desires to show mercy and grace to you when you sin so that you are empowered to live like Him.

"For what does the Scripture say? 'Abraham believed God, and it was accounted to him for righteousness.' Now to him who works, the wages are not counted as grace but as debt. But to him who does not work but believes on Him who justifies the ungodly, his faith is accounted for righteousness..."

– Romans 4:3-5

Abraham is called the father of faith. God came to him and gave him a wild and outlandish promise, but he still believed. He wasn't unaware of his own shortcomings or failures, but he believed in Him who justifies the ungodly. Abraham was ungodly when he started his journey. He was from the land of Chaldea, a place known for magic and idolatry. According to rabbinic tradition His father was an idol-maker.

It would have been so easy for Abraham, at any point, to stop believing in the promise of God because of all the sins he had committed along the way. However, what he had experienced in God was the ability to be righteous apart from what he had done. Similarly to Abraham, take your eyes off yourself and your own ability, and put them on Christ and what He has done. He is the one who justifies the ungodly. If you have lived an ungodly life, then this message is for you.

"...just as David also describes the blessedness of the man to whom God imputes righteousness apart from works..."

– Romans 4:6

Looking again at David's life, we see a testament of what it means to truly commune with God. David didn't connect with God on the basis of observing each law to the letter. As previously mentioned, David's life was anything but perfect.

It was his honest and vulnerable relationship with God that set him apart. David received a righteousness that wasn't available in the Old Covenant because he first connected with the heart of who God is: love. He became a man after God's own heart, certainly not by performance but through an undignified intimacy.

What David did in his lifetime was wicked. He committed adultery with Bathsheba and then crafted a wicked plan to cover up his sin and had her husband murdered. David's punishment should have been death—a life for a life. However, God blotted out his sin and allowed him to live. Psalm 51 records David's prayer to the Lord while his sin weighed heavily on him. He writes, "Wash me and I will be whiter than snow" (v. 7). David knew what He deserved, but he also knew the merciful heart of God. By believing that God was merciful according to His Word, David was saved from the death that he rightfully deserved. David was restored to right standing before God. The scales had been balanced. David received righteousness apart from his works, and his sins were forgiven by God!

David made some terrible mistakes, but ultimately, he still lived a blessed life. God still gave him victory, still let his descendants be the kings of Israel, and still brought forth the Messiah from his lineage. His sins did not disqualify him from being remembered as a man after God's own heart. God does not stop blessing us when we stumble. If He did, do you know what would happen? We'd begin to think that His blessing over us was due to our good behavior. We'd want to do good so we would get good from Him. We would begin to think, *I have all these blessings in my life because I earned them.* However, that is attempting to be justified by the law all over again.

Many people in the Church are actually afraid of getting blessed when they don't deserve it. We are equally afraid that someone is going to get more than they deserve, and the reason why is because we don't feel like we're getting what we deserve. "God, I did a lot more. I worked a lot harder. God, I should be getting more than this." We feel like our good works deserve a higher reward. That's how offense toward God can creep into our hearts.

Let me tell you something: I don't want what I deserve. And you shouldn't either! What we deserve is hell. Apart from Jesus, we deserve judgment and hell—that truth should humble us all. We're not deserving of any of the good things He has done for us. We never will be. He has chosen to be merciful to us because He wanted to show us mercy. Understanding this will make us more patient and loving toward others. We say, "Oh that pastor, who does he think he is coming back to minister after what he did? That televangelist. That so-and-so. How do these people fall and then think they can just get back up?" But God picks you up and restores you whenever you fall. Why should He do differently to anyone else?

Do you know what the problem is today? It's the same problem that was present in Jesus' day and in Paul's day. It's the same problem that the older brother dealt with in the parable of the prodigal son (see Luke 15:11-32). It's religion, and it puts you in bondage! It makes us glorify our own works above the free gift of righteousness. Religion doesn't allow us to celebrate when people around us get blessed. It detests mercy and resents free gifts of grace.

Relying on His righteousness and not our own has become a lost art. It opposes the religious mindset that keeps us bound to our own works. It frees us from our need to be right apart from Him and releases us to give glory to God for all the good things in our lives. Our boasting is in Him alone. When others succeed, we are able to celebrate because we know that God has more than enough blessings to go around.

When we see a young minister who has a huge following, another pastor might say, "I've been ministering for 30 years. I've been pastoring, I've been loving people, and this young buck who's 20-something years old just thinks he can do whatever he wants? That's not fair, God." What do we do? We start comparing and criticizing one another instead of cheering each other on. There is not a single person on the earth who could be good enough to please God without Jesus. We're all in the same boat. How can we destroy comparison in our lives? Through gratitude. We must learn to recognize that God has given us far more than we deserve.

Abraham was a sinner living in the Old Covenant, before Jesus and the Cross. Yet, even after making many bad decisions, he still understood and received the gift of righteousness by faith. If he could do that apart from the New Covenant, how much easier should it be for us now? He was willing to accept God on His terms even though he, by himself, wasn't righteous. All his life, God treated him as righteous. What does it mean for God to treat you as righteous? It means that in Christ, you are qualified! It means you are a partaker. It means the promises of God are your inheritance. The only question is this: are you in Him?

Stop seeing yourself as separate from Him. That is a lie from the enemy. There is no more separation or distance from the Lord. He doesn't come and go. He's here, and He's here to stay. You are a habitation, not a visitation. He gave His life so He could live in you.

Chapter Four

What Qualifies You?

In this day and age, everything revolves around marketing. From the time you wake up to the time you sleep, you are continually the target of someone's marketing campaign. The average person in America is exposed to anywhere from 4,000–10,000 advertisements *a day*. That's 4,000–10,000 moments we spend assessing the qualities of a product, the likelihood of us buying that product, and why that product is different from a multitude of others.

We have all seen filmed advertisements. The pitch may start with a well-dressed man or woman in a nice house. They tell you about how they spent years working for the best in their field, how they struggled with no money and yet made it to the top, and how what they have to offer is the very best. They share details about the product. No matter what they're selling, they are assuring their viewers that what they are selling is worthy of purchasing.

I am not demeaning these ads at all; in fact, I have made similar videos to promote books and online courses. I'm simply making the point that we buy what we believe will work, especially when we see that it has worked for someone else. Our beliefs are made clear by where we choose to invest our money. When you buy one cleaning product over another, you're communicating that you believe that the product you are buying is more effective than other options.

In the same way, we "market" ourselves to the people around us. We dress a certain way to communicate a specific message about what qualities or qualifications we have. For instance, you don't go to a mechanic and see them wearing a doctor's coat or a business suit. You're there because you need their expertise to fix your car. To find them pretending to be something else aside from what they are (a mechanic) would be bizarre.

The issue comes when we dress ourselves up in order to present ourselves to others, and even to God, as someone we're not. What if someone were to dress up in a nice suit and tell you they were very successful in business, but later on, you found out that they got the suit for free and they don't even own a business? You would call them a con artist. When we put on a show and act like we are doing better than what we are before God, we are doing the same thing. We're living in religion and deception.

Jesus addressed the Pharisees for doing the same thing. He said, "Woe to you, scribes and Pharisees, hypocrites! For you cleanse the outside of the cup and dish, but inside they are full of extortion and self-indulgence. Blind Pharisee, first cleanse the inside of the cup and dish, that the outside of them may be clean also" (Matt. 23:25-26). That's a sharp word from the "gentle Jesus" that people often think of. God hates self-righteousness. The times when Jesus was the harshest were when someone was making a claim to their own righteousness and their own qualifications.

Jesus came to justify the ungodly, the unqualified, and the unable. He had no sin but became sin so that we could, in Him, become the righteousness of God (see 2 Cor. 5:21). When you think that you can do enough to please God on your own, you're presenting a false image. That won't stand up before God, the righteous judge. Jesus is the only way to be qualified and remain qualified. You don't have the ability to perform well enough to be accepted by God, so you might as well quit trying!

That's just good news! It's not about you. The good news of the Gospel is the message that the apostle Paul was persecuted for. Paul lived a radical life. He suffered significantly for the Gospel. In 2 Corinthians 11, he says, "From the Jews five times I received forty stripes minus one. Three times I was beaten with rods; once I was stoned; three times I was shipwrecked; a night and a day I have been in the deep; in journeys often, in perils of waters, in perils of robbers, in perils of my own countrymen, in perils of the Gentiles, in perils in the city, in perils in the wilderness, in perils in the sea, in perils among false brethren; in weariness and toil, in sleeplessness often, in hunger and thirst, in fastings often, in cold and nakedness" (v. 24-27). Paul didn't suffer all of this just to spread around an updated version of the law, like the "Law 2.0." The message that Paul faced persecution for was that true fulfillment, rest, and qualification can now be received *outside of our own performance.*

> *"For I through the law died to the law*
> *that I might live to God."*
> *- Galatians 2:19*

Believing that your performance will never bring you rest forces you to rely on Christ's performance. That's faith righteousness. It's good news to find out that every promise God has given you, you are already qualified for. Take a moment to declare out loud: "I am qualified for the promises of God!"

Not only did religious people in Paul's day criticize and come against him for this message, but religious people today will do the same to *you*. Why? Because religious people do not want to accept Jesus as their righteousness. They want to work, earn, and perform for their righteousness. They want to make it about themselves and about what they can do. They don't want you to get rewarded when you don't deserve it because deep down they feel they are the only deserving ones. They don't want grace because they think their works are sufficient.

You may wonder, "What shall we say then? Shall we continue in sin that grace may abound?" (Rom. 6:1). Certainly not! I am *not* saying that sin is excused. I am also *not* saying that because He qualifies you, your actions don't matter and you can do whatever you want. What I *am* saying, though, is that God's grace empowers you to live a sin-free life. God's grace makes you righteous so you can bear good fruit.

Our problem is that we put the cart before the horse. We are called to do many incredible things, but we're called to do them them from knowing as born again believers, we are the righteousness of God. It is not, "Well I have to do this, this, and this and *then* I will be righteous." We wrongly think we have to bear good fruit *in order to* be righteous. It's the other way around!

Even as you are reading this right now, some of you are thinking, "Wait a second—I'm already righteous before I bear good fruit? That doesn't make any sense." Some of you have heard people say, "You have to be careful because if you hear too much grace, you're going to end up in sin. If you listen to too many grace teachers, you're going to end up in messes, because that's what grace does. It creates messes." Anyone who is saying something like that reveals they do not believe God's goodness and mercy lead to repentance (see Rom. 2:4). They are likely relying heavily on the fear of punishment to produce good behavior rather than believing that the free gift of righteousness and the abundance of grace can produce real, heart transformation.

> *"The sting of death is sin, and the strength*
> *of sin is the law."*
> *– I Corinthians 15:56*

As I have said before, it's foolish to think that hearing too many grace teachings will cause you to end up in a mess. What's the alternative? Is it hearing more messages about the law? No! The rocket fuel that gives strength to sin *is* the law. To say that teaching rules and regulations will make someone holy and righteous is heresy, and Paul calls it witchcraft.

In Galatians 3:1, he asks, "Who has bewitched you?" In case that's not clear, "bewitched" means to be lied to in order to damage a reputation, put under a spell, or be led away into error by dark arts. The context Paul provides for this bewitchment is found in the question, "Did you receive the Spirit by the works of the law, or by the hearing of faith? Are you so foolish? Having begun in the Spirit, are you now being made perfect by the flesh?" If someone is teaching that the way to make someone live like Christ is by submitting them to rules and laws, they are actively engaging in witchcraft and leading people astray.

If you could *(insert your favorite good work here)* enough to be right with God, then why would Jesus have ever needed to suffer and die? He could have just stayed in heavenly bliss and left us to figure things out on our own. The only way to live free of a sinful mess is to receive His grace!

"For the grace of God that brings salvation has appeared to all men, teaching us that, denying ungodliness and worldly lusts, we should live soberly, righteously, and godly in the present age..."
- Titus 2:11-12

Grace teaches us to live godly. Hearing grace preached is going to cause you to look more like God and deny all worldly lusts. Are you having an issue getting rid of an addiction, fear, excessive anger, or anything else you wrestle with? You don't need a law to tell you you're wrong—you need grace to empower you to be free. When you realize that you have been made a new creation, all the tendencies of your old way of life will fade away in the light of what God has done through you.

So, what are the promises that God has given you? Do you feel qualified to complete them? A God-sized promise requires a God-sized qualification. I find that because people don't understand their qualification in Christ, they don't dream big enough to change the world around them. God didn't just say go to of all your next-door neighbors and make disciples. He said go into all the *world*. We have to drop our own qualifications, our own track record, and our own ability. That is self-righteousness, self-serving, and self-centeredness. We must put off the old way of thinking and put on Christ. It's the only way to ever believe big enough to change the world.

Chapter Five

No More Egypt

Time and time again, the children of Israel saw God perform amazing miracles. He struck Egypt with plagues beyond imagination. He split the sea and delivered the Israelites through a passage of dry land. He provided them with water from rocks, bread from heaven, and clothes that would never wear out. He appeared as a fire to give them warmth at night and as a cloud by day to shade them from the desert sun. Every time opposition stood in their way, He turned their enemies away from them. There was simply no debating that the God of miracles was among them.

However, at the entrance to the Promised Land, the Israelites encountered a new problem. The Promised Land, the destination they had walked toward ever since leaving Egypt, was already occupied. And it was not occupied by just anyone, but by giants.

When the spies scouted out the Promised Land, they came back reporting that the land looked bountiful. However, the giants who lived there made them feel like grasshoppers. They started to wonder about God's plan for them. Could it be that despite what He had done for them along the journey, He brought them all this way to feed them to giants?

So there they were, standing near the Promised Land, wishing they were back in Egypt. Everything in Egypt was taken care of for them. However, they were *slaves* in Egypt! I can picture Moses having to plug his ears to block out the noise of the cries and shouts: "If only we had died in the land of Egypt! Or if only we had died in this wilderness! Why has the Lord brought us to this land to fall by the sword, that our wives and children should become victims? Would it not be better for us to return to Egypt? Let us select a leader and return!" (Num. 14:2-4). Isn't it interesting that when confronted with a problem they couldn't solve, they viewed slavery as preferable to freedom? Unfortunately, I think many of us today have the same mindset.

I love the TV Show *The Chosen*. I think it's a great depiction of the kindness and compassion of Jesus. When I watch these kinds of shows or movies, it makes me thankful that I am not living in Jesus' day and age. Yet, how many times have you heard people say, "Man, don't you wish you were there when Jesus walked the streets? I would love to have seen the person of Jesus. Wouldn't it all just be easier if Jesus was still walking around on the earth today?" Did you know that thinking like that goes directly against the actual *teaching* of Jesus?

If we're not careful, we can prioritize the life of Jesus *then* above the presence of Jesus *now*. Because He died and rose again, He now lives in us! He says in John 16, "It's to your *advantage* that I go away." Why, then, are we longing for something less-than? What are we doing? We're acting like the Israelites longing to go back to Egypt.

It's like saying, "Man, weren't things better back when we were slaves and all of our needs were taken care of for us?" We're longing for something in the past when Jesus is saying, "You're living in a better day. You don't need me to be a physical person to walk with you. Hello, I'm inside of you!" We need to get to a place where we stop longing for the physical manifestation of Jesus and realize that we are His hands and feet to the world around us.

We can confidently say that we have it better than ever because, when Jesus ascended, He sent us another helper: the Holy Spirit. The Spirit is the raw, creative power of God to accomplish His will on the earth. He is the complete manifestation of the character of God, given to us upon salvation. It is the Spirit that administers righteousness within us, which allows us to walk free from the power of sin and death. However, there seems to be quite a bit of confusion over the ministry of the Holy Spirit that has caused us to get bogged down and wish we had the person of Jesus still on the earth. So let's take a look at the ministry of the Holy Spirit and how it enforces and imparts the righteousness of God in our lives today.

"But now I go away to Him who sent Me, and none of you asks Me, 'Where are You going?' But because I have said these things to you, sorrow has filled your heart. Nevertheless I tell you the truth. It is to your advantage that I go away; for if I do not go away, the Helper will not come to you; but if I depart, I will send Him to you."

– John 16:5-7

Jesus explained to His disciples that they were sad because they didn't understand what was about to happen. He said that it was better that He went because then they wouldn't have to guess what He was thinking. Rather, His own Spirit would be living within them, teaching them, and explaining everything to them. They would have within themselves the very mind of Christ!

Imagine if you had Jesus walking around with you every single day explaining to you everything you needed to know, present in every choice. You don't have to imagine it because that is exactly what the Holy Spirit does for us! Let's read on:

"And when He has come, He will convict the world of sin, and of righteousness, and of judgment: of sin, because they do not believe in Me; of righteousness, because I go to My Father and you see Me no more; of judgment, because the ruler of this world is judged."

– John 16:8-11

This portion of scripture has led to some weird beliefs about the Holy Spirit. As we break this passage down, I have a few questions for you. Who was Jesus talking to in this passage? He was talking to his disciples. He says "because *they* do not believe in me." Who was He talking *about*? Unbelievers! "Because *they*"—unbelievers— "do not believe in Me." So yes, the Spirit does convict the world of sin, because the world does not believe.

However, does He say "sins" or "sin"? Sin. Singular. So, were there all these sins out there or just one sin? Just one! In reality, this isn't about the sin of abortion, the sin of homosexuality, the sin of witchcraft, the sin of idolatry, or all these other sins. There is one sin He was talking about: unbelief.

The moment you enter into true belief is the moment you transcend every other temptation and worldly entanglement.

So when you, as a believer, do something wrong, what is the Holy Spirit convicting you of? *Righteousness*! He's saying, "Hey! You're better than that! You're the righteousness of God, and you have the capability to live that out!" The Holy Spirit is not beating you down or reminding you of all the sins you've committed in your life. He's continuously working to form righteousness in your life! He's saying, "You're my child. I love you! You're better than that, and you're My very own righteousness. You represent Me. You don't need to deal with this anymore." This is why faith righteousness sets you free!

So, according to John 16, there is a difference between *being* righteous and *living* righteously. What's the bridge between the two? Believing. Knowing. Experiencing. The Bible says, "Be still and know that I am God..." (Ps. 46:10). The word "know" in the original Greek is *genosco*, meaning "to experience." Be still and *experience* that I am God. The more that you experience Him, the more you will believe in His righteousness. The more you believe in His righteousness, the more you're going to manifest it.

You will believe the truth, and the truth will set you free. It is not a matter of becoming introspective, dwelling on the past, and thinking, *Well, this happened when I was seven, and this happened to me when I was ten, and this happened to me when I was fourteen.* The past is over! The Bible says we are called to forget the past and to move on to the future of what He has for us (see Phil. 3:13-14).

"But now the righteousness of God apart from the law is revealed, being witnessed by the Law and the Prophets, even the righteousness of God, through faith in Jesus Christ, to all and on all who believe..."

– Romans 3:21-22

What we believe manifests in our actions. The passage says, "to all who *believe,*" not "all who do" or "all who act." Of course, the Bible does say we need to "do" and "act," but first we need to *believe.* When we teach people what to *do* instead of what to *believe*, we are going about everything backwards.

For instance, isn't it crazy how everyone knows Romans 3:23, and yet no one knows the verse right before it? We all quote, "For all have sinned and fallen short of the glory of God." This is true, but at the same time, why don't we know that this righteousness comes from God through faith in Jesus Christ to all who believe (see Rom. 3:22)? Notice that the verse doesn't say "to all who do." It's not "to all who act," "to all who are perfect," or "to all who do all these miraculous things." Rather it says, "to all who *believe.*" The reason why it is telling you to believe is that once you truly believe, you will produce it. When your beliefs change, so do your actions.

The question is, what do you do when your circumstances tell you something different? What happens when your life experience says there's still work to do? What happens when, like Israel, you've got a whole bunch of giants walking around in your Promised Land? The huge problem in the Body of Christ is that most people are able to believe in the finished work of Jesus right up to the point where their situations disagree.

Too often, when the going gets tough, people revert back to finding their acceptance and righteousness through their own actions. They start looking back to the slavery of the law—the figurative Egypt—and think, "Well, at least back there it felt like I knew what I was doing. Didn't the law take such great care of me? Wasn't it better when I just reaped what I sowed and didn't need all this faith?" After all, it does feel easier to believe that righteousness comes through our own actions. It is pleasing to our flesh.

The foundational building block of all sin is unbelief. It is the root that all other sin springs from. Unbelief separates us from the abundant life of God and plunges us into the trap of trying to prove ourselves. We resubmit ourselves to the world's system of merit and success thinking that outward progress is equal to inward security. *Because I'm doing a lot, I must be earning a lot.* This is why the Holy Spirit convicts the world of this one sin rather than the multitude of others. All the rest stem from this one thing. You don't have a pornography problem, an anger problem, a depression problem, an adultery problem, a gambling problem, etc. You have a belief problem. You don't believe Jesus paid to take all your problems onto Himself once and for all! And because of this belief problem, you are in bondage.

Sadly, this is the reality that many Christians live in. So many worldly Christians are still trying to prove their worth to God without Jesus. Maybe He was good enough as a sacrifice to get you in, but now you feel it's up to you. We try to reduce our spiritual experience to following formulas.

Because of this, there are whole communities in the Body of Christ that have come to a place of legalism, disappointment, frustration, anger, and bitterness. They're in this place because they worked all the formulas, and they did all the right things they were "supposed" to do and found out they don't work.

They're frustrated because they think that they're not getting what they deserve. They say, "God, I've given this much money. God, I've invested this much of my life. God, I've prayed this long. I've fasted this long. I've done this, and I've done that." Instead of turning back to a simple life of believing, they try their religious formula one more time thinking, *this time I know it will work*!

Have you ever been stuck in the formula trap? Are you stuck there right now? Are you running in a hamster wheel only to find yourself more and more exhausted? That's what happens when you make the Christian life about you. Then, when it doesn't work, what is your reaction? "Oh well, I guess I messed it up. I need to try again." It's not about you and your works. It's about what Jesus did and His finished work.

We need to start making this about what we *believe* instead of about what we do. I'm not telling you that your actions don't have consequences. Of course they do. If you kick a boulder, you're going to hurt your foot. That's natural logic. However, it's what God is able to do with your mistakes that makes all the difference. When you believe in the power of the Cross, your worst mistakes can be transformed into your biggest miracles.

Yes, it's important to hold people accountable for what they do, but the point is that if you don't change what you believe, it doesn't matter. If your mindset isn't renewed, it's just external behavior modification, and God is not interested in that. He's looking for heart transformation. You don't have to work, you don't have to strive, and you don't have to perform, because it's not about you. It's about Him and what He's qualified you for.

Chapter Six

Why Do You Want to Be Punished?

I have mentored many people over the years who have struggled with all kinds of issues. Struggles don't bother me. They're a part of life. To me, it's not about what they did but how open they are to let the power of Christ into their lives to change their situation. As a leader, people often come to me admitting their sins and issues, seeking forgiveness and help. Sometimes, the first time someone comes to me and admits a problem, I like to surprise them with my response. This isn't to make light of the situation but to break them out of the box of how they think God wants to deal with them.

For example, a few years ago, I was meeting with a student who had recently moved into one of our Grace Place houses. We didn't know each other very well yet, but as soon as we sat down, I could tell he was on edge and needed to get something off of his chest. After sitting there for a while, he leaned onto the table.

"Daniel," he said, "I need to tell you something."

"Okay," I said calmly, "What's up?"

"Well, last night I was on my computer. It was really late, and I should have been asleep. I ended up looking at something I shouldn't have."

"Okay," I said calmly again, "Thank you for letting me know."

A few moments of awkward silence passed. The guy stared at me looking confused and frowning. I smiled.

"Well, um," he stammered, "Aren't you going to say anything about it?"

"What do you want me to say?" I asked.

"I don't know, aren't you going to tell me what I did was wrong?"

"Do you need me to tell you what you did was wrong?" I responded. "Don't you already know what you did was wrong, and that's why you're telling me?"

I could tell my response was short-circuiting something in his head. It definitely wasn't what he was expecting. I didn't mind, though. I could tell this was good for him.

"Well yeah, but... aren't you going to tell me not to do it again or something?"

"I think you probably already know you shouldn't look at pornography or else we wouldn't be having this conversation. Do you need me to tell you that?"

The guy slumped back in his seat, staring at me in confusion.

"I don't understand." He said.

"Do you know what you're really waiting for right now?" I asked. "You're waiting for punishment. You're waiting for me to bring down the hammer on you. But I'm not going to. You know the truth. You know pornography is sin. Do your best to not do it again."

When we sin, we expect punishment. We wait for it. After all, we broke the law, right? That comes with consequences. But the truth of the Gospel is that our punishment has already been taken. It's true we *were* deserving of judgment and punishment, but it has been taken away.

> "But He was pierced for our offenses, He was crushed for our wrongdoings; The punishment for our well-being was laid upon Him, and by His wounds we are healed."
>
> - Isaiah 53:5 (NASB)

The judgment that we rightly deserved for being law-breakers was laid upon Jesus at the Cross. All of the punishment deserved was dealt with once and for all, and we walk free never to be found guilty again. Thank you, Jesus!

Let's be clear about something here: this does not mean that we can go do whatever we want. This does not translate into, *Oh, now I can sin as much as I want to!* That's foolishness, stupidity, and a misunderstanding of the purpose of grace. It is for freedom's sake that Christ set us free (Gal. 5:1). He did not free us from bondage just for us to put ourselves back under it. Paul says in Romans 6:1-2, "What shall we say then? Shall we continue in sin that grace may abound? Certainly not!" This good news that Jesus took our punishment doesn't mean we continue to sin; it means we are free to walk away from it forever! Isn't that amazing?

I want you to think about this. What happens when someone we know is in sin? What do we want to do? We want to put the law on them! Give them rules, strip away their privileges, micromanage them, and make sure they really understand the *weight* of what they've done. In other words, give them a path to *work* their way back into being in right standing again. Let's face it, we like laws! We enjoy working to attain something. The problem with that is that the strength of sin *is* the law. When people are in sin, they don't need the law, they need grace. Grace is what empowers people to be free from sin.

"For if by one man's offense death reigned through the one, much more those who receive abundance of grace and of the gift of righteousness will reign in life through the One, Jesus Christ."
- Romans 5:17

Those who receive the abundance of grace and the free gift of righteousness will *reign in life*. If the enemy knows that all we need to do to reign in life is simply receive the abundance of grace and the free gift of righteousness, what is he going to do? He is going to distort and attack the message in every way possible. What is happening to grace right now? It's being attacked in a way that it is being distorted, and the people who are distorting it are giving it a bad reputation. Therefore, the rest of the world is scared of it.

That's the enemy's plan! He whispers lies like, "Yeah, you got saved through grace, didn't you? Well, guess what? You have to work for it now. Did you commit that same sin again? There's no more grace for you. You used it all up. Yeah, you received that gift of grace, but it's not free anymore. You got saved through His righteousness, but what about working out your own salvation in fear and trembling before the Lord? Are you sure you've done enough?"

The enemy greatly desires for faith righteousness to remain a lost art. Think about how often he attempts to distort grace and righteousness with lies. This is why people are so scared of faith righteousness. What is the goal? To scare you back into the law. They get to a point where they ask, "Wait, how does being righteous by faith make any sense?" It makes sense because if you receive His abundance of grace, grace sets you free from sin. It makes sense because if you receive His free gift of righteousness, it's *His* right standing with the Father, not yours! When you're under the power of the law, sin is empowered in your life. When you're free from the law, righteousness is empowered in your life!

We need to know we are not called to be motivated by fear. Fear stands for "False Evidence Appearing Real." It is a lie we are fed to turn our hearts away from having confidence in God. It saps away our confidence, robbing us of the blessings that come through peace and trust. God does not speak to us or influence us through fear. He is the God of love and we, as His children, are called to be motivated by that same love.

Most people are afraid of God, and that's why they do what they do. They think things like, *I feel like I have to go to church because if not, God will be mad at me. Well, I feel like I have to give money because if I don't, God will be angry with me. I don't want to go to hell, so I guess I'll become a Christian.*

If you think that God is the source of your pain or your problem, whenever you need Him the most instead of running to him, you're going to run from Him. You're either going to want nothing to do with Him or try to work hard enough to win His approval. Both are dead-ends. Instead of looking to God as your answer and believing in the finished work of the Cross, you'll look at yourself and think, *What's wrong with me? What curse am I under now? What did I do wrong? Why am I like this? Why am I never good enough? Why are these people good and I'm not?* You'll start comparing yourself, which is a manifestation of law-based beliefs. On this road, you'll only find peace after outperforming the person next to you. However, it's a "peace" that will quickly fade. Comparison is a poor motivator and definitely not a fruit of the Spirit.

I'll say it again: the strength of sin is the law. The one thing that will leave you broken and keep you in sin is attempting to be made righteous by your own works. Nothing will keep you in sin as much as that. The more you try to be made righteous by your own works, the more you are going to make a disastrous mess.

"Christ has redeemed us from the curse of the law, having become a curse for us (for it is written, 'Cursed is everyone who hangs on a tree')..."
- Galatians 3:13

Christ has redeemed us from the curse of the law. Look in the mirror, point at yourself, and say, "You are free from the curse of the law!" I wish we would all believe this. Instead, whether we'd like to admit it or not, many of us treat our actions like karma, expecting backlash at the tail-end of every one of our mistakes. We do our best to perform our way out of these cycles and curses. However, in the end, it's just more striving.

Either Jesus' work was finished, or it wasn't. We have to get to a place where we know, beyond a shadow of a doubt, that we're in Him. "Therefore, if anyone is in Christ, he is a new creation; old things have passed away; behold, all things have become new" (2 Cor. 5:17). My question is this: Is Christ cursed? No. So why are we walking around thinking we are cursed? We have to know that our identity is found in Him!

We need to start living in a place where we know that nothing that is bad ever comes from God. We need to stop questioning ourselves and God. Whenever something bad happens, we need to run into our Father's loving arms. Psalm 91:1 says, "He who dwells in the secret place of the Most High shall abide under the shadow of the Almighty." I don't know about you but, when I was a kid, if anything bad happened and my dad was around, the "bad" wouldn't faze me. I had an amazing father who I knew loved me very much. I was confident because he was with me.

When you spend time with the Father in the secret place, you dwell in the shadow of the Almighty. You are standing in His shadow. If anything comes against you, guess what: He's your shield and buckler. He protects you. A thousand may fall at your side and ten thousand at your right hand, yet nothing can come near you because you're found in Him (see Ps. 91:7). You're one with Him.

It is time we stop letting lies and poor beliefs hold us back from giving our full trust and surrender to God. There is no safer place to be in the universe than in His arms. It's time we as His Body learn to question our perceptions of God instead of His character. It's time we stopped punishing ourselves and blaming God. Only when we see Him clearly can we begin to experience the true fullness of life that we were always designed to live in.

Chapter Seven

Blessings Are Not Wages

A pastor I know that was preaching a while back and a man arrived late to the meeting. The pastor was teaching about this same topic: identity, faith righteousness, and grace. The latecomer thought to himself, "Wow, this guy is a great teacher. I want to get one of his series." He wrote a check to the ministry and sent it with a letter that said, "Hey, I was at this event recently and really liked your teaching. I have AIDS, and I really want to get healed, so can you please send me a series on healing?" The letter arrived a few days later. The pastors secretary said, "Good morning, we just received a letter and a donation from this man, and he'd like us to send him a series on healing. Which one should I give him?" The pastor thought for a second and then, being led by the Spirit, said, "Send him the one on faith righteousness and identity." The secretary looked at him, puzzled. "Are you sure?" she asked, "He asked for one on healing."

"Yes," he replied, "I'm sure. Send him the one on identity." So the man with AIDS received their package a few weeks later, but when he opened it, he saw the series they sent him wasn't on healing. It was on faith righteousness and identity. He got offended. He got angry.

"I didn't ask for an identity series," he said, "I asked for a healing series. Who do they think they are sending me this? I sent them a check. I gave them money!" He was so frustrated that he put the series on his bookshelf and didn't pay any attention to it. It sat there on his shelf unopened. A couple of years later, as he was moving and boxing up all his stuff, he found the series.

This is that teaching series that minister sent me, he thought. Time had diffused his frustration, so he decided, *I might as well just listen to it.* As this man listened to the series, the power of God came upon him, and he felt energy and electricity going through his body. He thought, *Wow! I am experiencing the power of God! I feel different. I feel like God is healing my body. I'm going to go get tested.* He went to the doctor, and not only did he not have AIDS anymore, but he wasn't even HIV positive!

That's miraculous! Do you understand that is the power of the Gospel? Do you understand that no one even prayed for him? All that was necessary for him to be healed was in the Word of truth. However oftentimes what do we do? We say, "I need prayer, please!" We need to understand that the truth of the Gospel is enough. The truth of the Gospel is what frees us. You see people go overboard trying to get healed. They *perform* to get what Jesus has already paid for in His death and resurrection.

This is very different from the system we've grown accustomed to in the world. We are taught from a very young age that, "If you do good, you'll reap good in return. If you do bad, watch out, because it'll come back to you." What we learn is that whatever we have in life is due to how hard we worked for it. "If you have good things, congratulations, you deserved it. If bad things happen to you and you have had a bad life, you probably deserve it for the bad things you've done."

"Now to him who works, the wages are not counted as grace but as debt."
– Romans 4:4

Those who say that they're trying to get God to bless them or do something for them don't want a blessing. They really don't want a miracle. Do you know what they really want? They want a wage. They're wanting God to pay them for what they did for Him. They're thinking, *God, pay this debt you owe me. I prayed, fasted, and worked for this, so now you owe me. You owe me, God!* How many of you ever felt like you wanted that? *Come on God, I did this and this. You owe me!*

God doesn't owe us anything. Our own works of righteousness are worthless and a failed attempt to ease our own conscience. Jesus came to display an entirely different model for relationship with the Father. He came as a Son to reveal the Father. In fact, before He came, no one had seen the reality of what it meant to be a son. John 6:46 says that no one had ever seen the Father. They had seen the I AM. They had seen the Lord strong and mighty. They had seen Jehovah Nissi, Jehovah Jireh, and Jehovah Rapha. But they had never seen how to relate to God the Father as sons and daughters. Relating to God based on our own works will never get us anywhere. It's prideful, and God hates it. Relating to God as our Father, however, is the way that we experience all that He has for us.

This is the heart posture we want to have toward God. He is our loving Father, and we are His children. He doesn't bless us because we've done enough good works. He blesses us because we are His children whom He loves. One of the ways Jesus presented God as our loving Father was by explaining His desire to provide for us: "What man is there among you who, if his son asks for bread, will give him a stone? Or if he asks for a fish, will he give him a serpent? If you then, being evil, know how to give good gifts to your children, how much more will your Father who is in heaven give good things to those who ask Him!" (Matt. 7: 9-11).

It is His delight to provide for us and to do for us what we are powerless to do for ourselves. The issue that people have with this truth is that they haven't humbled themselves to really receive what God has already provided for them. The moment that you realize you are completely helpless on your own is the moment that God's strength, mercy, grace, and righteousness can move through your life.

I've had people come to me on the verge of burnout. They have been striving to be all that God has called them to be. They say to me, "I'm just done. I give up. I'm quitting this!" I tell them, "Great! Now maybe God can take over and do what He wanted to be doing in you all along." That's the message of the Gospel.

You couldn't do it, so He did it. You couldn't earn it, so He earned it on your behalf. You couldn't do enough right, so He lived a sinless life for you. You couldn't go long enough without giving up and doubting that God had called you, so He persevered through death. He then rose again and ascended to the right hand of God. Now we step into all He did for us. It is finished. He's already done everything for us. So now we just believe and live in His grace, love, and freedom.

"For His divine power has bestowed upon us all things that [are requisite and suited] to life and godliness, through the [full, personal] knowledge of Him Who called us by and to His own glory and excellence (virtue)."

- 2 Peter 1:3 (AMPC)

John 1:12 says that as many as believed and received, they had been given the right to be called children of God. When we believe the Gospel, we enter into a personal relationship with God. In this belief, we realize that He loves us and gave His life so we would know Him. In relationship, we come to realize that He has already given us everything we need in life. We no longer have to turn to our own dead works to provide for ourselves, but rather receive all that God, our Father, has already provided for us. The Good News is we aren't under a curse, but now we're blessed in Christ Jesus. When we walk in this understanding, we'll realize that provision is all around us, and we have what we need right where God has placed us.

Do you know that every time you try to ask for something, you're telling yourself that you don't have it? Think about it. Why do you ask for things? Because you don't already have them. If you had it, you wouldn't need to ask. That's why, when I pray for healing, I don't say, "God, will you please—"; I say, "God, thank you for—." The price has been paid. It is finished. Our prayers should be so full of thanksgiving that we should sound like this: "God, thank you for this, thank you for this, and thank you for that." If someone heard us and didn't understand what we were doing, they would think we had won the lottery!

"I write these things to you who believe in the name of the Son of God so that you may know that you have eternal life. This is the confidence we have in approaching God: that if we ask anything according to his will, he hears us. And if we know that he hears us—whatever we ask—we know that we have what we asked of him."

- 1 John 5:13-15 (NIV)

If we know that He hears our prayers and we are praying according to His will, then we can rest in the confidence of knowing we have what we ask for. I have so many testimonies of favor and receiving wildly luxurious blessings. I always have more than enough because it's Jesus' favor, not my favor. At the end of the day, I truly believe that much of what I experience happens because I'm training my mind to thank Him for all the things I'm receiving. I'm thanking Him for blessings before I receive them because I know He's bringing them to me.

Let me say it again: as long as you're trying to get something from God, you're reminding yourself you don't have it. If you're trying to qualify for it, you're saying to your heart that you're not qualified for it. The man that had AIDS let go of his offense. He decided to stop trying, to stop performing, and to stop earning. He decided to follow the truth of the Gospel. Matthew 6:33 says to "Seek ye first the Kingdom of God, and His righteousness; and all these things shall be added unto you" [KJV]. He sought God's righteousness and perfect health was added unto him. Instead, many of us seek first *our* righteousness, but the scripture doesn't say that! It's all about Christ and *His* righteousness! It has nothing to do with us at all because we were co-crucified with Him on the Cross!

Chapter Eight

Are You in Christ?

When you walk into most bookstores, what is one of the biggest sections? Self-help. When we listen to Christian radio, what is most of what we hear? A self-help message. Self-help is a multi-million dollar industry. *The Top 10 Ways to Make Yourself Look Better, Feel Better, Be Happier, Etc.* Think about this: why are we trying to get help for something that was supposed to be crucified? Why are we trying to fix our broken hearts when God has promised to give us *new* hearts?

Our culture is obsessed with trying to make things look better, sound better, and seem better than what they really are. The common misconception is that as long as you look successful, you are successful. However, in Christ, there is a different and greater reality at play. When we read these self-help books and listen to these messages, what are we telling our hearts? *Yeah, the Cross was good but it wasn't enough, and I need to add to the finished work. Yeah, Jesus finished the work for other people, but He didn't finish it for me. I have to continue to do, do, do.*

What this reveals is that people think being in Christ is not enough. They believe that Jesus gave us a starting place, but now we have to figure out righteousness and holiness for ourselves. You will always be caught in the rat-race of works and the law until you realize that *you* have died, and it is *Christ* who is alive in you.

> *"Therefore, if anyone is in Christ, he is a new creation;*
> *old things have passed away; behold,*
> *all things have become new."*
> — *2 Corinthians 5:17*

I have some questions for you. Read these slowly and note your response.

Are you perfect?

Think for a moment and answer honestly. Read the question again. Write your answer in the margins of this book or on a note. Once you've done this, read the next question.

Are you perfect in Christ?

Maybe this question feels a little easier to answer. My guess is that most of you responded more readily with a "yes." Why was it easier to respond yes to this question versus the previous one?

Are you in Christ?

If you've given your life to Jesus, this one should be easy. Yes! Now, let me ask you the first question again.

Are you perfect?

When I travel and preach on faith righteousness, I often ask these questions. When I ask most people if they're perfect, at first, they confidently say, "No." I ask if they are perfect in Christ, and most will say, "Yes." Are you in Christ? Anyone who's read the Bible will say, "Yes." Then, I ask the last question and watch the looks on people's faces as they start to grasp what I am implying. Some people start laughing at this point, and others get offended. If the last question offended you, it's time for a shift in perspective.

Why are you separating yourself from Christ? It's easy for us to think, *Oh no, I'm just a wicked, wretched sinner. I'll never be perfect.* Let me be very clear. You're either in Christ, or you're not. We can develop ridiculous mindsets to try and come to terms with problems in our lives. The mindset can be so ridiculous that we justify our problems. People think, *Well I'm in a church meeting, so I'm in Christ.* Then after church ends, they think, *Now I'm stepping into the world for the rest of the week, so I'm stepping out of Christ.* That's ridiculous! That mindset is from the enemy! He's trying to keep you blind so that you don't live in your identity in Christ.

When you realize that you're in Christ, you see that whatever is true about Christ is true about you. Jesus is favored, so you are favored. He is blessed, so you are blessed. He was anointed with the oil of gladness, so you are too! As He is in this world, so are we (see 1 John 4:17). He is righteous, holy, and blameless, seated at the right hand of the Father, fully accepted, filled with light, walking in wisdom and love. So are you! Christ came and destroyed the works of the enemy, and so will you! Christ came to set the captives free, bind up the brokenhearted, and declare the year of the Lord's favor (see Is. 61:1). You are called and fully equipped to do the same. The only gap between you and that reality is faith. You need to have the faith to declare "I am in Christ!" every single day.

How do we find out whether or not we have that faith? Simply by looking into the Word! Did you know the Bible has a test in it to let you see if you're living in faith? We find the "Faith Test" in 2 Corinthians 13. This test is either pass or fail, and you take it every day (most don't even know they're taking it). Are you ready to take it?

Let's start with verse 5:

"Examine yourselves as to whether you are in the faith. Test yourselves..."

Here's the glorious truth about the faith test: We're called to examine *ourselves* as to whether we're in the faith! Well, how do you do that? It says to "test yourself." And how do you do that? Let's continue:

"...do you not recognize this about yourselves, that Jesus Christ is in you—unless indeed you fail the test?"

The faith test is this: every day you're making a subconscious decision. You either think, *I believe and know that Jesus Christ is inside of me,* or you do not. That's it! You're either walking in faith, knowing Jesus is alive and active within you, or you are walking in ignorance by not being aware of this reality. One mindset leads you to live a life full of the power of God and righteousness. The other leads you to act as though you're separate from Him whenever you fail. One leads you to live in the truth and the other leads to deception.

The truth of the Gospel is that you can't get any closer to God because He already lives inside of you. He is living in you, through you, and *as* you (see Gal. 2:20). People say, "Wouldn't it be great to be in the Garden of Eden with Adam and Eve? They walked with God!" Why would I want to go back to that way of living? Why would anyone desire to go back to a time when God was only on the *outside of mankind*? How much greater is it that He lives inside of you? We are trying to get something that we have already received! We have uninterrupted communion with God inside of us, which is more than Adam and Eve had.

There's an amazing book by Andrew Wommack titled, *You Already Have It (So Quit Trying To Get It).* On the cover, there's a Dalmatian chasing its tail. This is a great analogy for when we cry out to God and ask Him to give us things that He has already given to us. Many well-meaning believers pray for God to come and fix their issues. Every time I hear someone pray like this, I say to myself: "God is sitting on His throne and saying, 'What else do you want? I gave you My best! I gave you My Son! I've given you all things pertaining to life and godliness. I've given you the keys to the Kingdom. Why are you trying to get Me to do other things instead of taking your rightful place as sons and daughters on the earth? I've given you dominion. I've given you power. I've given you all things! Stop believing the lie that you are limited, and start believing that I live inside of you and because of Me, you can do all things."

Some people say, "Oh, but Daniel, you don't understand. I'm still under the curse. I'm still under this problem and that problem. If you saw how limited I really was, you'd understand." Where in the Bible do you see Jesus saying this? Where do you see anyone in the New Testament say this? Never. Stop believing these lies. They're the enemy's strategy to cause division between you and other people. These lies are attempting to prevent you from living out your identity in Christ. Some of you are so hard on yourselves and you don't even realize it. You've normalized trying to achieve, earn, and perform so much that it feels weird or wrong *not* to. If you realized what you've *already* been given, the toil would cease.

The law is the strength of sin. When you were born, you were born with a sin nature (see Rom. 5:12). When you had that nature, it would be normal and natural for you to live in fear, unbelief, and sin. Unless you accept righteousness as a free gift, you will continue to live out of your sin nature—even if you've been born again! We see this happen all the time. People may choose to accept Jesus as their Lord and Savior. However, if they're not accepting Him as their righteousness, they're going to keep living out of their sin nature, just like the Judaizers did thousands of years ago! They'll keep offering sacrifice after sacrifice, convincing themselves that Jesus might have died for them to get to heaven... but not to live free from sin.

We have an epidemic in the Church in the form of carnal Christians: believers who are still living out of their sin nature. This is why the majority of the Body of Christ believes they still have a sin nature. This is why sin is so prevalent in the Church. What you believe about yourself is what you will manifest. If you believe you are a sinner, you will inevitably sin by faith. However, if you believe Jesus has taken away your sin nature and nailed it to the Cross, what do you think will happen then? If you believe that Jesus is your righteousness and therefore you are righteous, how in the world can you continue to live in sin?

Before you got saved, did you ever do anything good? Of course. Have you ever carried someone's groceries out to their car for them? Were you ever respectful to your parents? Yet, at that time, you were a slave to sin. You were a prisoner to your master, sin. Your chains were your past, addictions, fears, substances, doubt, hopelessness, and more. You were bound to the limitations of a normal, fallen man. Nothing you did was good enough, and you were stuck in the never-ending rat race of trying to become but never arriving. You were bound in your carnal nature.

Let me ask you a question. Did any of those good things you did ever get you out of that prison of sin? No. Of course not! No good deed could have ever set you free from your sinful nature. No holy act could have ever made you right with God. So why would you think that any wrong decision would get you out of the prison of righteousness you are in now?

You didn't get yourself into the prison of righteousness by your works. You simply believed in the finished work of the Cross. You were transferred by Jesus from the kingdom of darkness into the Kingdom of light. If you didn't get yourself in by good behavior, why in the world would you ever think you could get yourself out by bad behavior? It's not about you or what you did. It's about Him. It's about His righteousness. It's about what He did for you and your choice to receive the free gift He has made available for you. You are free from sin, so stop trying to get free. You are free from limitations, so stop trying to get out from under your limitations. You are free from every lie of the enemy! You are free to live in Him.

The Gospel is so much more than a story we tell on Easter and Christmas. It's the power of God to invade and transform every area of your life. It's the power that takes the limits off and rockets you upward into the high call of God. The Gospel is that you are righteous, not by your own works or ability, but by the work of the Holy Spirit living through you.

You didn't do anything to earn the Holy Spirit or His righteousness. In fact, you did as much as humanly possible to disqualify yourself from it! And yet, God still came to the earth, in the form of a man, with His mind set on redeeming you. You have access to righteousness you could never have gained for yourself. You can live free from sin and compromise. This is the power of the Gospel! This is the power of the resurrection of Jesus!

I dream of the day when the generation I'm living in raises children in a grace-filled and supernatural culture. I long to see all the truths I've written about become normal so that we don't need to keep re-laying the same foundation over and over again. I dream of the day when our children know from an early age about His righteousness and the supernatural. My hope is that by the time they are 19 or 20 years old, they will be mighty men and women of God. I dream of a generation in which revival is normal in both our beliefs and our lifestyles.

To get to that place, we have to make the decision to walk in the freedom and truth of the Gospel for ourselves. After all, how can we expect anyone to learn something that has become a lost art if we aren't there to resurrect it? We need a transformation in our own thinking to shake off the chains that religion and bad beliefs have put us in. We cannot change the world by trying harder. We must believe something greater.

I hope that this book has challenged you in some way to rethink what you believe about your relationship with God. I hope that you are inspired to pursue a righteous lifestyle, free from the curse of sin and death. Living in faith righteousness doesn't have to be a lost art. Jesus paid a high price for us to walk in total victory, and it is time that we, the Church, make the decision to walk in it.

Pray this with me as we conclude:

God, thank you for the free gift of righteousness! Thank you for sending Jesus to fulfill what I never could on my own. Father, I receive your grace today. I receive your righteousness and reckon myself established in the heavenly nature of Jesus Christ. You paid the price for my freedom, and I'm not under the curse any longer. I'm under your blessing. I'm in your grace and favor. I live in your freedom. No matter where I go or what I do, I am righteous by faith in Jesus' name!

"...And the just shall live by faith."
- Romans 1:17

About Grace Place

Grace Place Ministries is a discipleship community fueled by a passion to see God's people walk out their identity in Christ and establish His Kingdom upon the earth. We are committed to developing mature Christian leaders through one-on-one mentoring, building family through weekly gatherings, and providing leadership opportunities designed to facilitate connection and growth. We travel frequently to minister around the world and create resources to build up the Church in her righteous identity.

—————————

Vision

Mature sons and daughters
established in their identity in Christ,
spreading the Gospel of grace and truth.

Mission

Disciple young adults.
Minister around the world.
Resource the nations.

Discipleship is our Mission; Will you Join Us?

Now, more than ever, the body of Christ needs to arise and shine. The world is searching for answers and is in need of an encounter with God's love and truth. Who will raise up a generation to bring answers our world is desperately seeking?

"For the earnest expectation of the creation eagerly waits for the revealing of the sons of God."
– Romans 8:19

Whether it is a young man or woman needing a mentor or an entire church seeking the resources to disciple their community, you can make an impact!

Become a Partner
with Grace Place Ministries:

Go to:
WWW.GRACEPLACEPARTNER.COM

Grace Place Ministries

ADDITIONAL RESOURCES

THE LOST ART OF DISCIPLESHIP
God's Model for Transforming the World

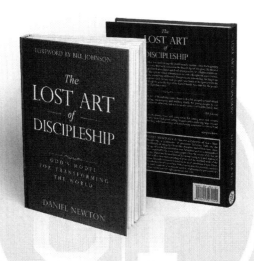

Discipleship is not a man-made idea. It is God's design for world transformation. *The Lost Art of Discipleship* is the uncovering of heaven's blueprints for remodeling the kingdoms of the earth into the Kingdom of our God. In his cornerstone book, Daniel Newton pulls from 20 years of experience in discipleship. As you read, prepare your heart to be ignited with the fires of revival that once swept the globe as in the days of the Early Church. It is time for the people of God to arise and shine for our light has come!

Available at www.GracePlaceMedia.com

@GracePlaceDiscipleship

Additional Resources

The Lost Art of Discipleship
Workbook

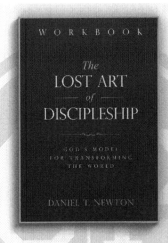

Enrich your understanding and increase your mastery of God's model for world transformation. This companion workbook to *The Lost Art of Discipleship* book is filled with exclusive content, in-depth exercises, and practical coaching to introduce a lifestyle of discipleship in your day-to-day walk. Whether you have been following the Lord for years or recently surrendered your life to Jesus, this manual breaks down the Great Commission and equips you for a life of fruitfulness!

Available at www.GracePlaceMedia.com

@GracePlaceDiscipleship

ADDITIONAL RESOURCES

THE LOST ART OF DISCIPLESHIP
Online Course

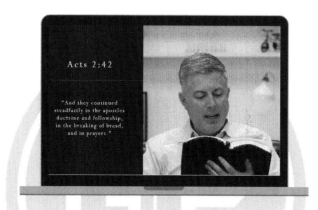

You can live the Great Commission. Every believer is called to embrace Jesus' final command: to make disciples... and this interactive online course is designed to take you even deeper into the rich content taught in *The Lost Art of Discipleship*.

Whether you are wanting to position yourself as a son or daughter, lead as a father or mother, or create a culture of discipleship, this course is for you! Rediscover the lost art with over five hours of video content, practical teaching, quizzes, and supernatural activations from Daniel Newton.

Available at www.GracePlaceMedia.com
@GracePlaceDiscipleship

Additional Resources

Immeasurable
Reviewing the Goodness of God

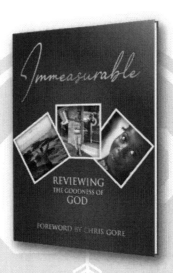

You are made in the image of the Miracle Worker,
designed to manifest His glorious nature.
Immeasurable: Reviewing the Goodness of God is a collection
of 100 real-life stories of salvation, healing, deliverance,
signs and wonders, reconciliation, and provision. Every
miracle is a prophetic declaration of what God wants to
do in, through, and for someone just like you.

Additional Resources

Truth in Tension
55 Days to
Living in Balance

Never Give Up
The Supernatural Power of
Christ-like Endurance

Other Titles

The Lost Art of Perseverance
Rediscover God's Perspective on Your Trials

All Things
Have Become New, Work Together for Good,
Are Possible

It Is Finished
Exposing the Conquered Giants of Fear,
Pride, and Condemnation

Available at www.GracePlaceMedia.com

@GracePlaceDiscipleship

Additional Resources

GP Music: Beginnings

Everyone has a story. Most people don't realize that God doesn't just want to improve their story. He wants to rewrite it. Beginnings offers a fresh start, a new focus. This worship album invites you into the core anthems of grace and truth which have impacted us at Grace Place.

Our prayer is that this album helps you lay down your past mistakes, your present circumstances, and your future worries in order to lift both hands high in surrender to the One you were created to worship. We ask that you join us in a new beginning — an exciting start to a life filled with perseverance, focus, and surrender.

Available at www.GracePlaceMedia.com

@GracePlaceDiscipleship

KEEP US UPDATED

We would love to connect with you and hear about everything God has done in your life while reading this book! We also would love to hear how we can be praying for you. Submit a testimony or prayer request by going to GracePlaceRedding.com/mytestimony

STAY CONNECTED WITH GRACE PLACE

Are you interested in staying up to date with Grace Place Ministries and receiving encouraging resources via email?

VISIT OUR WEBSITE:
www.GracePlaceRedding.com

SIGN UP FOR OUR NEWSLETTER AT:
www.GracePlaceRedding.com/newsletter

FOLLOW US ON SOCIAL MEDIA:
@GracePlaceDiscipleship

Made in the USA
Coppell, TX
11 December 2022

88788819R00048